Bill Smith is a political scientist and writer from Belfast, educated at the University of Sussex and Stanford.

During Northern Ireland's "Troubles" he worked for the Department of Health as a social policy administrator supporting community action, and for the European Commission on cross-border cooperation.

Since then he has served as a member of the Parliamentary Boundary Commission and as Chair of the Early Years Organisation.

Most of his previous writing has been in official or academic language. In 2011, the US Institute of Peace published his analysis of British policy on Northern Ireland, *From Violence to Powersharing*. In 2021, he co-edited *The Idea of the Union* (Belcouver Press).

He celebrates this, his first printed volume of poems, as a step forward in the journey of personal liberation which began when he retired from full-time employment thanks to a medical condition in 2004.

He is grateful to the Arts Council of Northern Ireland for its financial support.

IRREGULARITIES

WILLIAM BEATTIE SMITH

FLYING DOG
PUBLICATIONS

Published 2022
by Flying Dog Publications

Except as otherwise permitted under the Copyright Designs
and Patents Act 1988, this publication may only be reproduced,
stored or transmitted in any form or by any means with the prior
permission in writing of the publisher or, in the case of reprographic
reproduction, in accordance with the terms of a licence issued by
The Copyright Licensing Agency. Enquiries concerning reproduction
outside those terms should be sent to the publisher.

Copyright © William Beattie Smith 2022

ISBN 978-1-3999-1722-3

Designed by Rosie Smith

Printed by April Sky Design, Newtownards

for Mary and my children, partners in irregularity

"… Now that my ladder's gone,
I must lie down where all the ladders start,
In the foul rag-and-bone shop of the heart."

Yeats

Contents

Foreword by John Wilson Foster

I was surprised to learn of Bill Smith's poems. I have known him for a very short time and only as a fellow-editor of others' ideas and as a writer of political opinion. And I know, too, that he was a distinguished civil servant, an habitué of committee rooms, a writer of memoranda and reports. Though by his own account, he was encouraged by two superiors to be as eloquent as these dry genres of writing permit. A far cry, even so, are these largely fugitive verses that compose *Irregularities* from the previous uses of his pen — or rather, as he tells us in "Finding a Pen", the uses of his previous pens.

This is not unique, of course, and many a lyric poet has been a civil servant, but the incongruity remains and prompted my surprise.

Still, a minor and mischievous connection might suggest itself as one reads "Commissioners" in which the chief commissioner takes the chair and eyes in the room glaze over. Perhaps the glaze in one sitter's eyes camouflaged a creative and preoccupied doodling, as it were, that was the germ of that night's poem. The doodling that decorates the verses in *Irregularities* is equally inspired and fitting and shares a playful and deceptive inconsequence with the words on the page.

Moreover, immediately the poems are under way, Bill is as attentive as his committee assignments and his political writing demanded. He is simply paying close attention to different things. Not to agendas, motions, or five-year plans; not to political interpretations or historical explanations, but to images of the real and ordinary world. This is where Ezra Pound thought poetry began — with the capture of the hard and vivid image, quite the opposite of abstraction, analysis and opinion. In "CJ turns 40" the image is retrieved from "a bokeh of flowers/pink yellow cream/behind you the Victorian conservatory". "Bokeh", I learn, is the effect of blurred background lights in photography. In this poem it is also the past which the poet wants to bring into focus with an urgency that inspirits this slim volume for sad reasons that become clear.

The images are snapshots that become for the most part brief vignettes and usually of what Patrick Kavanagh called "the commonplaces of life", including family memories. These are not so much smelted in the Monaghan poet's passion and "raised up to angelhood", as shyly acknowledged as mysteries or miracles which the haiku-like miniatures are shortcuts to signalling. (See "Two Monkeys", "Inner Life", "After Heine".) The apparently trite or trivial — the daily, casual and close-at-hand — can deceive, for as Kavanagh reminded his readers, "gods make their own importance".

In any case, the poems' subjects and tone are in stark contrast to the planned, the predicted, the consequential and weighty, or the done deal. In the course of a life, the civil servant and statesman can lose their souls and betray their earlier selves ("Peer Review", "Memoirs of a Statesman"). This contrast is played out at any moment and is the role that the incongruous, the oblique, and the unforeseen play in our existence.

Life ambushes life and *Irregularities* captures the small moments of subversion or sudden distraction. The poet's reading the memoirs of an important man (and memoirs are usually the politician's ordering of his career by hindsight) is interrupted by a robin's alighting on his shoulder, a surprising happening at least the equal of the memoirs in importance, it's implied, and a mute irony. Surprise animates these poems. If I was surprised to learn of Bill's poems, he may well have startled himself by writing them.

His verses suggest he has found himself surprised by something this side of joy. And I suspect that such surprise was not in the plan, which was a taking stock by someone who senses Eliot's eternal Footman.

This album of free verse is an ill man's testament. And the regrets, the things not done, are part of the ledger though more than offset, it seems to me, by the credit column of humour, irony and above all love, and the implied and modest consciousness of a life that has acquitted itself well under the circumstances.

To steal from Dr Johnson: a person's sudden awareness of mortality "concentrates his mind wonderfully" and reading *Irregularities* has caused me to give new meaning to the good doctor's adverb. And to hope that these poems, good as many of them are, are in the bigger context actually five-finger exercises, a learning of the ropes, a limbering up for competitive leaps on days to come.

John Wilson Foster
Sidney, British Columbia
January 2022

A Message from our Patron

Take time to savour these poems
Read them aloud and share them with your friends
May they touch, move and inspire you

Writing

Composition

this is not toothpaste
squeezed from a tube

it is a humming-bird
which almost landed on my wrist

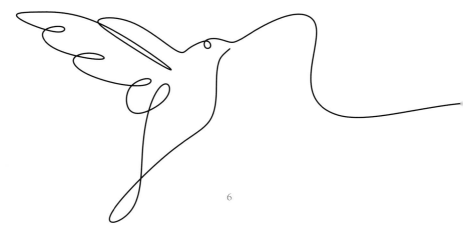

Anima

"Why would you want to do that?"
the celebrated poet asked in amazement
"It's torture and a waste of time. Think again."

yet unexpectedly at seventy
I am learning the words and ways
of a new lover
who caresses me and whispers in my ear
when least I expect it

I need to know what she is like in bed
what she likes in bed
what engages and intrigues her
what makes her laugh
what secrets she has to tell and teach me
what is tabu to her
what bores her
what irritates her
what distracts her

conversations that will never end

Expert

the respected professor
offers me advice
do this, do that, follow the great man
or you will fail

professor, you offer not love but dominion
do not take it amiss when I proceed
as I had intended
junking your guidance

Abundance

I sing a song of abundance
the wonder of walking
the stretch at the back of the knee
the eye flying forward
all that occurs

Finding a Pen

Coming up to my first recital
for family and friends
I worry for a week

afraid of rivalry and failure
would they think me ridiculous
for calling myself poet?

I choose my pieces carefully
light with dark
some playful some intense

I ask for feedback making it safe
not a performance but a consultation
not the slow unpeeling of my heart
but an exercise in craft.

They listen laugh and cry
Rosie gives me cakes
Nad tells parrot jokes

I open up
I will not close down again
kindness is all

I have found a pen

Silence

Better than 1000 useless words is one single word that gives peace

Inner Life

people are never quite right for me
or I for them
I watch life from the edge

After Heine

how sweet it is
doing nothing
then taking a rest

Two Monkeys

two monkeys chatter together
a frog plops into the pond
what are they saying?

Family Album

Incarnation

My dad kept a diary
in a lined A5 notebook
one square per day

for my birth he wrote:
"Junior (Billy) arrived at 9:00 o'clock this morning
both excellent"

there followed seven days of snow

my next recorded event was
"Billy fell head first into his wardrobe"

Solo Race

ramming the pedals
the boy roars round the lawn
scattering gravel

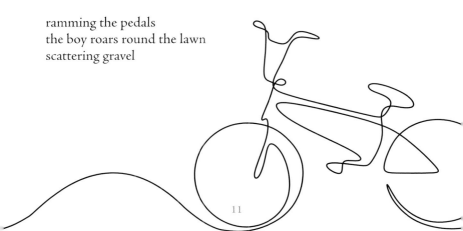

Eden Lodge

tennis court, apple orchard
Tudor beams, oak stairs
ladies' lounge, servants' kitchen
smell of varnish

home

My Sister

I threw a tennis ball
at my little
sister's head

over and over
it bounced off
her face

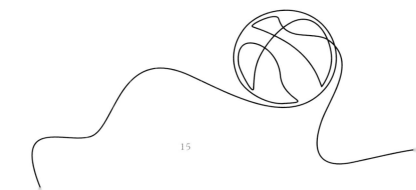

Uncle David

my bronzed uncle
clever David
back from his travels
sits by the fire
in my dad's chair
cravat to the throat

stretches across
my mum's dainty sandwiches
helps himself
to plump mushroom patties

Uncle Purvis

My happy uncle Purvis
swung me by the arms
wheeeeeeeeeeeee
we played with a ball
on the grass
as the ocean blew
strong and sweet and clear

then he married
a woman called June

The Night my Granny Died

my mum and dad went to see her
leaving me alone

I took one of my mum's
cigarettes from her blue Wedgwood box

smoked it in the garden
my rite of passage

Grandad's Moustache

my grandad's moustache was not cool
aged three I sat on his lap

on the baggy brown trousers of his pinstripe suit
taking in his gold-plated watch-chain

my mother invited me to stroke his moustache
(why would she do that?)

I did not want to, but I did
it was old and grey and tobacco-stained

big like a walrus's
brittle to touch

the clock ticked
he did not smile

Big House

Mum sold the big house
we grew up in
dumped the lounge suite
on the lawn
stuffed the bridge table
in a skip
went to live
by the sea

diabetic now
she sits by the window
inside the rain
munching chocolate gingers

CJ turns 40

When I search our lives together
memory glazes over
only snatches recur
and quickly dissolve

I resort to photos
find you cheerful in your high chair
dribbling beans

then proper – grown up
in your new school uniform

holding your rigid baby sister
an angel framed in marigolds

sitting with your big sister
serious with long blond hair over studious glasses

at Granny's for Christmas
in a silver paper crown

close-up with short bleached hair
kind eyes smiling for the camera

then come phones to capture the moment
your face as it is
standing out from the blur
hair cropped at the sides
waved on top
as you munch on salad in a bistro

last is the portrait
you chose for your website
professional now
doing what you love

around you a bokeh of flowers
pink yellow cream
behind you the Victorian conservatory

I am happy and proud of you
eyes alive as you turn to the sun
in your tweed cap

these images endure and we are whole

Adolescence

PE Girls

When I was eleven
mum took in lodgers
two young women
from the college of physical education

Bea and Paddy
made me happy
they laughed and glowed

but dad disagreed
he removed the fuses from their fires
forbade them to eat oranges in their rooms

French Girls

for my first trip outside Ireland
I visited my pen pal
in the country near Paris
her name was Arlette

her family had a pet rabbit
who lived in a hutch
on a little bed of straw
we ate him for lunch

her dad gave me chores
emptying the incinerator
removing used tampons
which had not burned

Arlette had a friend
Giselle from Beirut
who lived in a big house
with a walled garden

Charlie Fay

My grammar school was four grey blocks
the north housed Classics
Dr Fay guarded its core
it smelled of chalk-dust and fear

I spent two years
with agreeable lazy masters
basic grammar, simple words
the layout of a Roman house

in year three we moved to Fay's dread realm
he gave us each a Latin name
I was Faber meaning Smith
he taught us scansion, dactyls and spondees

trembling behind wooden desks
translating Caesar and Cicero
Virgil and Horace
nowhere to hide

he would screw a knuckle
into the hollow over your ear
if you were cheeky
he would hit you on the head with his fist

I once translated a poem
and pinned it on his board:

"I do not love thee Doctor Fay
the reason why I cannot say
but this I know that anyway
I do not love thee Doctor Fay"

my classmates read it at break
Fay found it
moved it
said nothing

borrowed our essays from the teacher next door
scrutinised our handwriting
reached no conclusion
for I had used my left hand

on my next term's report he wrote
"Good but not as good as he thinks he is"
my mum found this amusing
shared it with my wives

later at university I saw Fay
knitting woolly hats at a lecture
again in the street I met him
lifting dog turds to drop in a bucket

he spent his holidays
performing translations of Latin plays
donating the proceeds to orphans in Vietnam

Public Life

"The State is the embodiment of Reason" – Hegel

Memoirs of a Statesman

I sold my soul to the state
now it's too late

Peer Review

Lord Pugh
as an angry young student
railed against the regime
marched for working-class unity

is now a celebrated historian
advisor to Ministers
he sits in his suit
in the Peers' Dining Room

reading The Times in silence
beside him his wife Lady Pugh

Commissioners

The Chief Commissioner takes the chair
eighteen eyes glaze over

Chairman of the Board

"Destiny moulded me for this job"
he said: and melted
into his pinstripe suit

Mandarin's Dream

clacking through star-dappled streets
in a long linen nightgown
two knobbly knees
on my way to a meeting
which I am to chair

knowing nothing

when I arrive
I am wearing
child's leggings
with moo-cows and stars

Speech

the audience settles
the Minister opens his mouth
a waiter drops a plate

Memoirs

sitting quietly
reading the memoirs
of a very important man
a robin settles on my chair

Springtime in Italy

Hose

she has laid a yellow plastic hose
across the entrance to my room

"Hullo", she says,
"It's a lovely day!
Are you going to sit there
huddled in the cold?"

Cat

two little girls in pink
play in the garden
a brown cat runs up a tree

Guilty Pleasure

sitting in the sun
sipping a cocktail
watching strong men dig
stripped to the waist

The Master

he was taking wine with me
on the terrace explaining
his plans for the building
the decline of education
corruption in public life

his wife came and asked
whether he was in fact
going to help her clear the brambles

which soon after he did

01hyyy99zx

I sit at my table
transcribing aphorisms
a plump ginger cat purrs in
laps from my tumbler
tiptoes across my keyboard

Hillside

I walk up the hill
behind the house
to the chapel ruins

lie on the grass
suck in the sun
listen to the silent sky

Death

sitting in my room
outlining thoughts on death

my pen runs out of ink

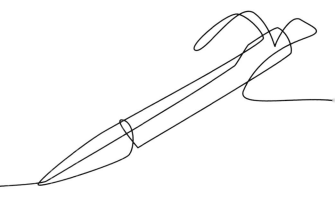

Midwinter blues

Selling the Baby

As soon as Hallowe'en is over
the merchants begin selling Christmas

they feed on the need for ritual
they feed on the yearning to belong
they feed on centuries of tradition
they feed on the myth of the baby in the manger
living in poverty an outcast

a miraculous birth that changed the world

Heart of Christmas

Once I believed in Santa
woke before dawn
emptied my stocking
ran downstairs to tear open presents
electric train, model cars
atlas of the world

I married and had kids
Christmas made sense
the midnight service with candles and carols
Jesus placed into his crib
sherry in the drawing room
sitting beside my dad at dinner

as he carved thin slices of turkey and ham
setting fire to the brandy on the pudding
fancy liquors in crystal glasses
the youngest child proud to be chosen
to hand out the presents
one at a time while everyone watched

once the wrappings had been tidied away
dad would light his pipe
I a small cigar
the kids would go to the playroom with their toys
we would sit companionably together
dozing in our armchairs

at six, mum would amaze us back to life
with a trolley of tea and sandwiches
it was all too much
but we ate it anyway
until the children grew tired
and we went home happy

the year my marriage broke up
a miserable feast
late dinner dry turkey
drinking too much
chewing in bitter silence

cups were thrown and we argued in bed

then my dad died, genial host
carver of meat and lighter of fires
who chose to be cremated
the rooms grew chill, the dinner mediocre

turns out his silent presence
all along
had been the heart of Christmas

Plague

Certainty

everyone is worried
"will I catch the Covid?"

probably not
but even if you don't

you **will** die

Soft Beings in Hard Times

They say we are living in hard times
stuck behind our doors
can't meet or touch or hug
how is life to go on?

I'm old now, nothing works as it should
my prayer is for the coming people
the hopeful voyagers
pursuing their dreams

for my children, planning a wedding in the sun or bringing up babies
in love and hope
standing by one another when the grey wall looms
confident that life's green wires will thrive

three beings sustain me
Mary my love who strains to keep me well
Strega the pup who barrels at my beard
and the house we share

every thing in its place

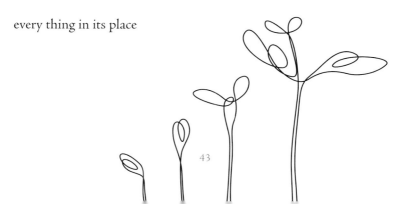

Flashes

Morning

flat on my bed I lie
you bring me coffee in a green cup
a tiny sun glints into my eye

Attendant

for over an hour
a fly has been standing
on my kitchen window pane

Kitchen Sink Drama

robin dances in grass
stabs bread
cat coils

I bang window
cat crouches
bird flies

Wasp

I sprawl face down on my blanket
a wasp has died there
tiger-fierce, skull face, wings erect

Love

The Science of Love

call it love or call it projection
call it soul or call it brain
both work

Desire

she puckers her lips
tang of a woman's flesh
flowering open

Eye Traction

his ancient eye sucks her body in
it pleases him
unlike her character

Lanzarote

she breasts the blast
braving the ocean's crash
naked as the day she was born

Love of my Life

I can't put you into rhyme
you live and breathe beside me
inside me and around me
our homes are one

we anticipate each other's words
say the same simultaneously
compete over crosswords with caustic curses,
end each day with a tender caress

when the ice-curtain falls between us —
as sometimes it does —
I howl and hide, forsaking the world
waiting for my sun to shine again

when it does I dance
happy in the light of your lasting love

Treat me Special

I don't want you
to buy me cake
and call me sweetheart
I want you to want to fuck me

I don't want you
to slacken and mutter to yourself
I want you to sing and dance
and come with me at the moon

I don't want you
to be nice and tell me you love me
I want you to squeeze me and listen to me
and make me feel special

Dogs

Little Red Dog

little red dog
round brown eyes
curled ensign tail

greets me when we meet
leaps up and paws my legs
rolls on his back for a stroke

pricks up his ears
grins through broken teeth
shows his tongue's pink tip

he is not brave
scuttles sideways from shadows
cringes from trucks

but he is dutiful
defends his bitches
bristles and barks

Manny

the velvet touch of an old dog's paw
tells me this is home
always has been

Porridge Eyes

I puckle porridge
in the pan
two eyes watch me
hungry hound

Bone

I gave my dog a bone
now I am reborn
a breathing skeleton

Death

Sex

if only I had had
more sex with more people
when I had the chance

Living

we are not waiting in the waiting room
we are dancing in the garden

Concern

I stand in the shower jet
warm water soothes my skin
from below I hear a knocking

Bone Cancer

Old frog croaking in the reeds

aware he is dying
the old man decides
to gather his scribblings

something is going to happen
he doesn't know what
the end of him is death

the hand that gripped the wheel
now hangs limp
thwarted by a pot of jam

who will be home for Christmas?
children and grandchildren
will I still be here?

this is how it ends

I creep away from the feast
muttering apologies

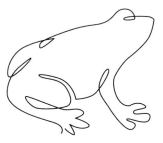

Jag

my Jag is big and strong
it whisks me in style

when I put my foot to the floor
it cuts through the countryside
a flash of grey steel

if something goes wrong
with a bearing or strut
I can pay a man to fix it

unlike me

Last Christmas

the leaves are beautiful
colours of fire
dropping from the branches
piling up on the lawn

the apples are rounding
plump for Hallowe'en
children squealing with delight
Christmas will be next

celebrating rebirth out of the hard earth
new life will stir
they mark the turning as best they can
with gifts and decorations

no rebirth for me
the final winter is coming
climbing stairs drains me
the coldness in my bones is here to stay

Lights Out

some very old people may live after me
probably David Attenborough will
being a well-loved naturalist

but my life is easy now
breathing, eating, sleeping
two pairs of slippers by the door

my tooth broke at the root the other day
may not need it long
but a kindly dentist agreed to fix it

will my dog miss me?
she may sniff my socks and wonder briefly
then fetch to someone else the rope we used to tug

gold and crimson leaves
swirl in the breeze
snowdrops quicken in the earth

new slippers arrived today
too bright and stiff for me to wear
someone else may have their use

nightshirt on
teeth cleaned
lights out.

Saying Yes

the poet Larkin says that being brave
lets no one off the grave
death is no different whined at than withstood

I neither withstand nor whine
my death may seem premature
interrupting plans and upsetting loved ones

but that's how life ends for dogs and men
more certain than the wavering beginning

I look back from the terminus and say
"if only I had said Yes more often"

Where is the Bad Thing Going to Happen?

in me

in my bones and blood and brain
they tapped me to test it
sucked fluid from my spine
chiselled through my hip bone
drilled out a cylinder of marrow

the question is when

Battling Cancer

my doctors are on my side
my body is their battleground
carcasses impaled on barbed wire
the rotting flesh of marvellous horses

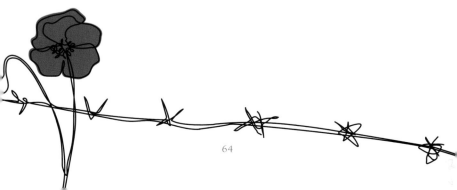

My Tears are Bigger than Yours

this thing I am dying of is scarier
than that thing that you are dying of

I have cancer in my blood and bones
it could spread to my brain and bowels

my grief is bigger than yours
all you think you have lost is an illusion

but my life is a tragedy
you are a narcissist, I am a victim

Dying

what is the best death?
slipping off quietly in your sleep
or dropping the body during meditation

it may be a kindness before then
to have a gradual transition
autumn shading into winter
shedding desire and ambition

no longer wanting to have more
do more
travel more
make more friends

what I fear is not total emptiness
— I have that every night —
but the decline turning against me
losing the use of my hands and legs

unable to drive cars or open jars
trapped downstairs
can't dress myself
incontinence and vomiting

can't think straight
needing strangers to care
who may be neither kind nor caring
ostracised, undrinkable tea and mush to eat

expected to be grateful
going mad with no one to complain to
nothing to look forward to
tomorrow will be worse

better the death of Felix Faure, president of France
caressed to death at 58 by his mistress
skilful courtesan Marguerite Steinheil

Designing a Death

my doctors tell me I have a terminal illness
if I could die of something else
what would I prefer?

there are no online reviews
no Google Death or RIP Advisor
I have to decide for myself

I imagined having enough time to settle my affairs
but that will not happen

will I drop the body in the night
or lose the power of thought and linger?

which is better, sudden or slow?
what if I don't get to say goodbye?

and think of all those stanzas
unfinished and unstarted…

De Mortuis Nihil Nisi Bonum

just because you are dying
doesn't make everything you say OK

In the Void

after is the same as before
only I am not

so what?

END

Afterword by the Poet

At the age of 71, I did not take on lightly the project of publishing my first volume of poetry. Who was I to presume to being a poet when others — like my former English teacher Michael Longley — had devoted their lives to the service of the Muse? I had written a few poems and some memoirs but had never seriously considered publishing them.

Most of my written work had been policy papers for the civil service: advice to ministers, press releases and minutes of meetings. There was a discipline to all these documents: they had to be succinct, factual, and balanced.

Until the mid-1990s, their quality was guaranteed in my Department by the fact that they were overseen by literate men of principle who loved language and logic: the classical scholar Norman Dugdale and Senator Maurice Hayes. They showed me that it was possible to be literate and skilful in the administration of public affairs, and that the civilising virtues of the humanities are essential to the craft of good governance.

In many of the poems in this volume I have tried to catch a fleeting sensation, emotion, memory or event: a one-off irregularity. The longer poems build on these to create more complex pictures. I wanted each poem to be short, light and concentrated; musical and rhythmic; emotionally engaging; free from fixed formal structure; and written in everyday language. I wanted to avoid references which required a university education to understand, redundant words, similes, metaphors, advice and moral judgments.

The overall structure of the book — loosely a chronological memoir preceded by an introduction on my approach to writing — may be viewed as an anti-memoir, directed against the self-promoting autobiographies of important people. This is most evident in the section "Public Service". With underlings hanging on your every word, it is easy to take yourself too seriously and exaggerate your achievements. The tone of these memoirs typically begins energetic, hopeful and ambitious. After a decade in the system, the hero has reached the middle rank and is ruthlessly pursuing his ascent. By the time he reaches the top he is drained of feeling. He no longer tells impish anecdotes but boasts like a press release of his key role in historic events.

If I have devoted more attention to death and dying than to the earlier phases of my life, that is because this is my present reality. In February 2021 my doctors at Belfast City Hospital diagnosed that I had acute lymphoblastic leukaemia, the long-term consequence of chemotherapy two decades previously. This can be controlled by medication but not cured. I suffer from tiredness and breathlessness. My wonderful haematology team at the Belfast City Hospital keep me alive with regular blood transfusions. I am grateful to them for every extra day.

My diagnosis forced me to confront my own mortality as an immediate possibility. This gave a new urgency to my creative work. After decades of writing about the outer world, the time had come to explore my inner landscape and talk to the beings who live there.

Acknowledgements

I want to thank the people who gave me material for the poems in this volume, which I have gleefully used without their permission; my partner, Mary, who gave me the space to write, encouraged me, assessed my work as I produced it and improved it; and my children, who positively encouraged the eccentricity of publishing a first volume of verse at 71. Jamie supported me in having my first two poems published online (by Cephalopress) and diligently edited my work; Rosie converted a 70-page Word document into the work of art you are looking at now; CJ provided moral support and wise guidance from when I began to write; and Anna, as Artist in Residence at Flying Dog Publications, contributed greatly to creativity, writing and design. Finally, cultural commentator Professor John Wilson Foster understood the magnitude of the transformation in writing style which I had undertaken and through his solid endorsement helped to bring it about.